ART ADVENTURES IN NARNIA

BY

SHARON JEFFUS

copyright 2006

This book is dedicated to Carol Hubal who has encouraged me so much!

Introduction

I hope this book allows children and students everywhere to exercise their God given ability to be creative and do original thinking. Francis Schaeffer, the great Christian apologist, said "The Christian is the one whose imagination should soar beyond the stars." Einstein said "Imagination is more important than knowledge." Techniques and art history are incorporated into these lessons, but creativity is paramount. Websites are given for maximum learning. I do recommend seeing the series of Tolkein movies and the new C. S. Lewis movie. They are excellent! As much as I can research, Narnia was a real country in ancient history. With the imagination, C. S. Lewis takes you to an imaginary place full of wonder and intrigue. Many great life lessons can be learned from fantasy writing. Parables have long been used to teach truths of life. These books, as any story, teach us lessons on how to live our life. My hope and prayer is that this book might encourage young people to realize the visual effects that bring a written story to life. The book *The Lion, The Witch and The Wardrobe is* in three forms. It can be read, it can be watched in a cartoon version, and has a couple of movies made that tell this amazing story. Allowing children to write and illustrate their own book is a wonderful idea. To take it a step further, you can allow them to make a storyboard and film their story with a home camcorder. This is the first step to becoming familiar with how to tell a story in video, a primary source of today's communication, especially to the younger generation.

Art Credits:
I want to thank Dannielle Diehl for doing some original pencil sketches for this book.
I want to thank Michael Helm for doing the cover of this book.
I want to credit the art work of Richard Jeffus that was used in this book.
Sharon Jeffus also did several of the drawings.
I want to credit the Dover Historical Archives and Borderbound Click Art with several of the historical images.
I want to thank Jonathan Jeffus for his expertise in computer art.
I would also like to thank Dr. Jim Thompson, for his encouragement to write again.

Table of Contents

ASLAN

The Peaceable Kingdom

One of the great things you see in the *Chronicles of Narnia* is the wild lion tamely lying with lovely children in peace and strength. One of the most famous pictures that shows this is "The Peaceable Kingdom" by Edward Hicks. There are over 100 different versions of this famous picture. Hicks, an itinerant preacher, painted this picture and gave it as a gift to his parishoners as the peace that he wanted to see between the settlers and the Indians.

One of the greatest lions ever created in art history is the masterpiece lion by Rubens in the following art work. Go to this website to find out about Rubens and look at this mighty lion <http://www.scribbleskidsart.com/generic221.html>. This is a lion done in preparation for his painting, "The Lion Hunt." Do you think he captured the mighty power of a lion? Could you use this picture as inspiration for your picture of Aslan? In the Bible you hear about the Lion of Judah. There are many different names for Christ. Can you think of some? If you were going to compare the person you admire the most with an animal, which animal would you choose and why?

In the picture above, do you think the anger of a lion was captured in the artist's drawing? Notice the eyes. How did the artist get the eyes to look angry?

When drawing the head of a lion, begin by putting basic shapes on your paper lightly in pencil. You will find that once you get the proportions on the paper, you can then add details. The difference is in the details. Notice all the fine lines in the two drawings on the left. Notice the dark areas and light areas.

Do you think the lion above looks like a patient lion?

The lion above is made by just using lines. Copy this lion.

M. C. Escher has a very famous picture of birds changing into triangles. Go to this website to see it: <http://www.etropolis.com/escher/scroll.htm>.

In the Bible the dove is the symbol of the Holy Spirit. The lion is the lion of Judah. In C. S. Lewis's story, what animal can you combine with the head of the lion to show some of his great character?

In the picture above, we see the bird changing gradually into a fish. This is just a very interesting thing to do in art. It is metamorphosis or change. Just as a caterpillar goes to sleep in a cocoon and comes out a beautiful butterfly, when we give our hearts to Jesus, he changes them. Can you think of something else that changes as it grows? How about a tadpole becoming a frog, or a baby becoming an adult. Do a picture of an animal at the beginning stages of growth and change it into something else. Fantasy art sometimes takes different creatures and combines them into one make believe character. An example of this is a centaur; half man and half horse.

Drawing Lions With Ages 3-7

When little ones are making lions, you can use these simple steps to help them make their lion. They can use basic shapes to form their creature. Fine motor skill activities are fringing paper for the mane of the lion and drawing lines out from the center to form their mane. Make their lion roar and teach them the letter R by making a series of R's that get larger and larger for the roar.

For the project above use a paper plate and yellow paper for the mane. Use a paint stick or craft stick and glue on the mane. Whiskers can be pipe cleaners.

Art elements that children can learn making lions are **hot colors**. Lions are usually yellow and gold. Black is a **neutral color,** and whiskers and eyes can be black. A sandpaper tongue can be used to reinforce the word **texture.** Always say the names of the shapes when drawing such as **square, rectangle and circle.** When you are drawing always use the words **vertical, horizontal and diagonal** when making these lines. Have the children repeat the words as they draw.

You need yellow construction paper, scissors, glue, black construction paper and markers. You also need sandpaper for the tongue. Reinforce the word **texture.**

9

Draw your creature in the space below.

Creating a Creature

A wonderful art activity with students is to make a creature that has never been seen before. Within this framework, you teach that it must rest on the **horizon line;** the place where the sky and land meet. It must have **shading, shadow and texture** in the picture. It must show **scale**. This means that you must put something in the picture that will show what size the creature is. The finger in the drawing above above shows that the creature is very small. Make sure that you teach **foreground** and **background** in the picture. This allows students to learn not only vocabulary of the arts, but they must be creative and show original thinking as well.

Heraldry:

Lions were used on many of the flags and shields throughout ancient and medieval history. You can make a shield by taking a piece of cardboard cut into the shape of a shield. Use white craft glue and take heavy yarn or rope and outline the shape of a lion on your shield. Let this dry. Cut aluminum foil into 2 inch squares and use white craft glue and cover your entire shield with these squares. When this is dry, rub black tempera paint over the entire shield. Rub the paint off with a damp rag. Leave some black on the shield. Let this dry and varnish the shield. It will look like old metal. The lion will stand out from the surface. This is **two-dimensional art.** If it was **three-dimensional art,** it would look like a lion as you walk all the way around it.

Parting of the fields was when the **artisan** (person who makes the shield) would take the shield shape and divide it into parts. On each part he would have a symbol of the idea of the shield. On the shield above, we see four main pictures. If we made a shield of Narnia, and the lion would be the main character; what would you put in the three squares at the top of the shield?

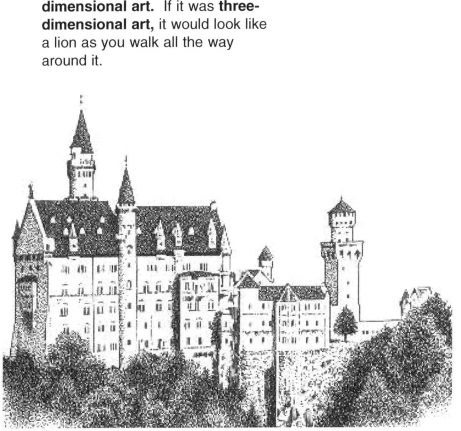

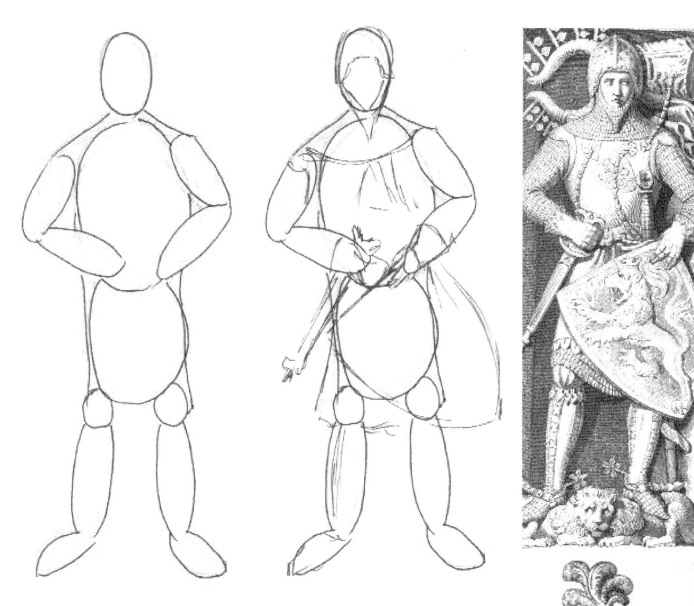

Above you see the process of drawing the high king. You add more details in every phase of the drawing. **Shading, shadow and texture** make the figure look real. Draw Peter. Beneath Peter is Edward. Draw Edward.

Types of Armor

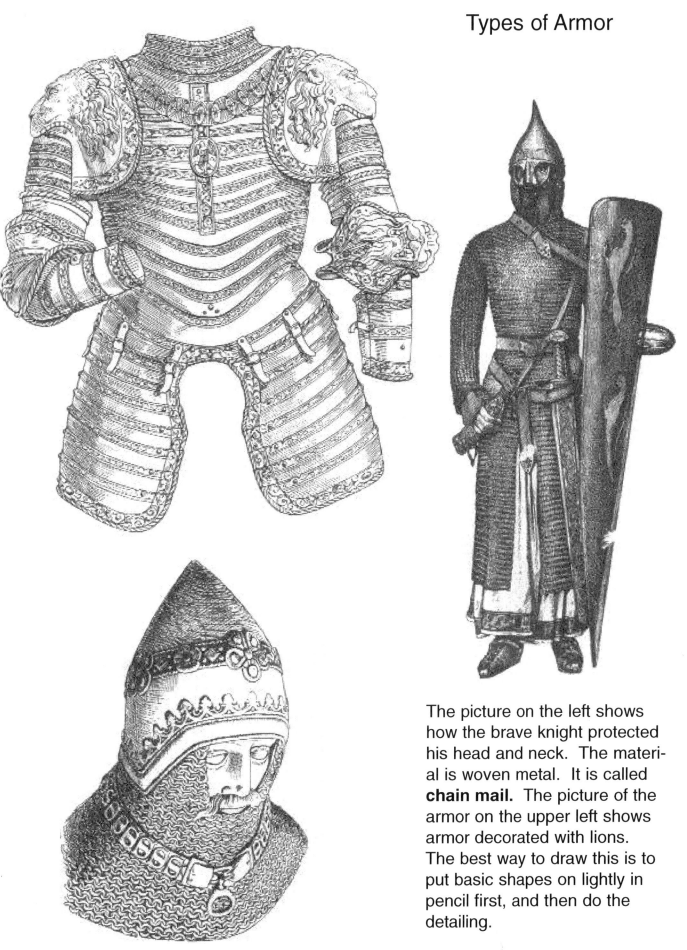

The picture on the left shows how the brave knight protected his head and neck. The material is woven metal. It is called **chain mail.** The picture of the armor on the upper left shows armor decorated with lions. The best way to draw this is to put basic shapes on lightly in pencil first, and then do the detailing.

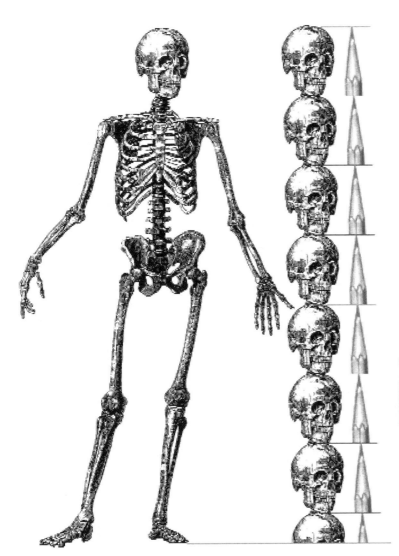

Football players of today are like our warriors of yesterday.

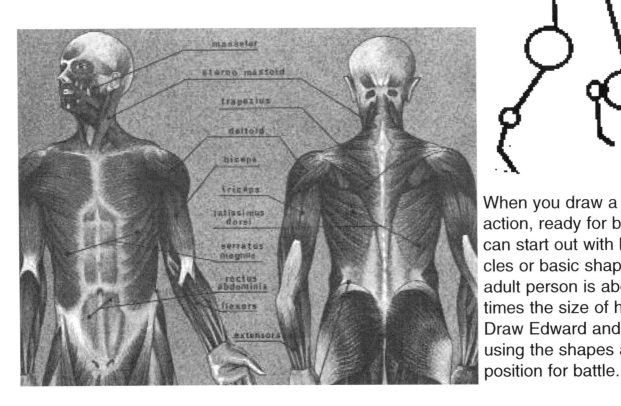

When you draw a person in action, ready for battle, you can start out with lines and circles or basic shapes. Each adult person is about 7 1/2 times the size of his head. Draw Edward and Peter just using the shapes above in a position for battle.

When drawing with younger children, always verbalize **vertical, horizontal and diagonal line.**

Use the two top drawings to show how to draw King Peter. In the drawings on the left and the right, emphasize **pattern**. Making the small circles on the coat on the right develops fine motor skills.

Ancient Weapons

Ancient weapons and armor are always exciting to study and see. Try to design a sword for battle. Swords are always marks of honor for a soldier. In all of Tolkein's trilogy and C. S. Lewis Chronicles, you see battle scenes. In the Bible, you read that we are soldiers if we are Christians and we need to wear the armor of God as seen in Ephesians 6:10. The color wheel is an important concept in art. Draw a soldier and put each part of his armor a color of the color wheel.

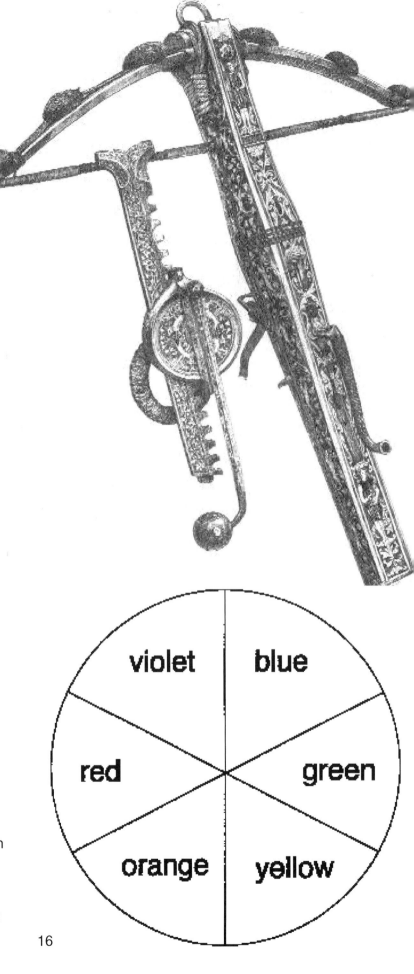

Sculpey is a good medium in which to design a sword head. You can bake it, paint it, and glue gemstones on it. A **sculpture** is something that you can go all the way around; make sure your sword head looks good from every angle.

violet | blue

red | green

orange | yellow

16

Helmets and Crowns

This might be a helmet worn by a great warrior. There are two wonderful internet lessons on making a helmet:
<http://www.clemusart.com/kids/art/haveago/armor.html>
http://www.kidsdomain,com/craft/hall-knight2.html

A crown can easily be made of cardboard. You can even use the same technique that you used with the shield to make it look like metal. You can purchase gem stones at your local discount store and glue them on.

Draw your soldier in the space below.

Lightly make the following shapes to define the shape of a lion's body.

Add shading on this lion's nose, and shade the legs on the left. Remember that **shading, shadow and texture** make things look real.

Li..

Draw the lion above using the circles below. Draw them lightly in pencil first.

A Lion Throne:

When we picture the thrones at Cair Paravel, we can picture one similar to the one on the left. You can see the lion at the top of the throne. The thrones probably contained many precious stones. Use the diagram at the lower left and build a chair base using posterboard and white craft glue. Go to your local discount store and purchase felt, gemstones, etc. to glue on your finished throne. One idea is to make the throne very ornate and put wings on the back. Could you make the throne look like a lion?

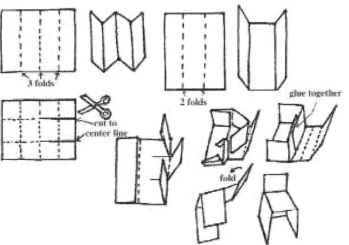

3 folds

2 folds

glue together

cut to center line

fold

21

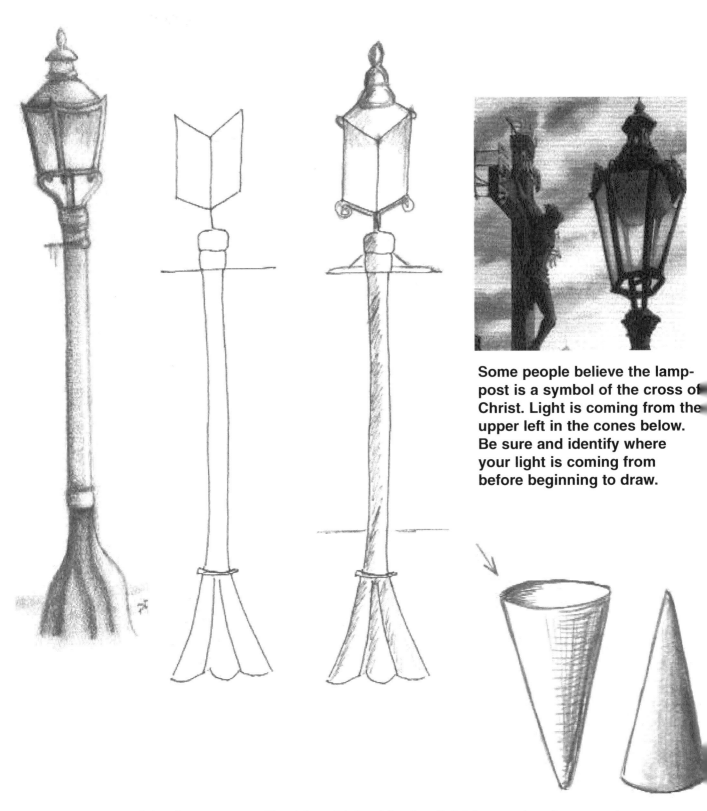

Some people believe the lamp-post is a symbol of the cross of Christ. Light is coming from the upper left in the cones below. Be sure and identify where your light is coming from before beginning to draw.

Draw a picture of the lamp-post. Decide which side the light is coming from and then shade it according. Remember there are different kinds of shading. You can shade by **smudging** like the first lamp-post, or you can use **stroking** like the third lamp-post.

Inside the Professor's house:

One of the greatest pictures of a room is done by the master artist Matisse. Go to this website to see his picture< http://cgfa.sunsite.dk/matisse/p-matisse2.htm>. Notice all the patterns in this picture by Matisse. Here is a picture of an interior room in the professor's house. Things in the **foreground** of the picture are larger. Things in the **background** of the picture are smaller. What items can you mention that follow this rule? Color this room in rich and dark colors.

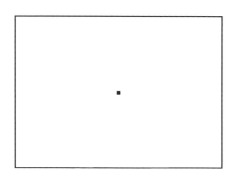
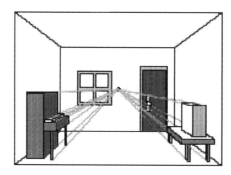

On the previous page we see that things in the **foreground** are larger and the **background** are smaller. Things are in correct perspective. Use your imagination and draw the room that contained the wardrobe.

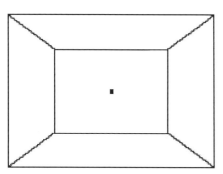
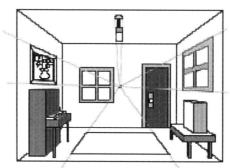
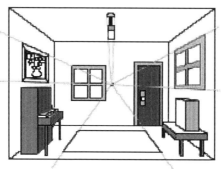

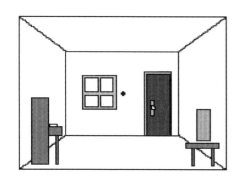

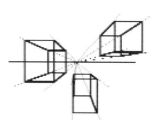

A good art project is to take a rectangle of brown bag paper and cut a line up three quarters of the center and then cut 2 inches on either side. Fold these doors you have created to look open. This is your wardrobe. Put **patterns** on the outside of the wardrobe. Students can draw the wintry land of Narnia in between the doors. They can also decorate the room in detail.

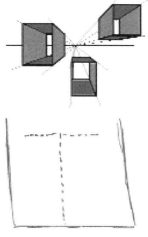
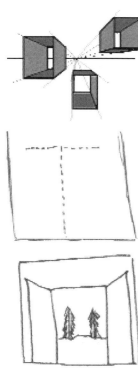

Notice on the right how the bannister is a **one point perspective**. It gets smaller and smaller as it goes back.

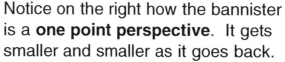

Trompe l'oeil is a picture of an illusion. It is centuries old and uses **perspective** and **shading** to create an illusion. Base relief columns and vaulted ceilings use this method. It would be if you went into a room and looked at a picture and it looked so real it looked like you could go into it. The picture below is of a window back into the age of dinosaurs. It uses one-point perspective and shading to make it look real. Do a door into a wintry land.

A wonderful project idea to teach **foreground** and **background** is to have students do a picture of something far away. This could be the witch's castle or the stone table. Have them put the scene in the snow. Have children cut out the picture and glue it on the front of the piece of art. These creatures will then be covered with snow, as will the whole picture. They are much larger so that is the **foreground**. You can rub on white tempera paint or use Q-tips for snow. Another good idea is to cut out the flowers and put them on the front of the picture, as indications that Aslan is on the move. The idea is to get students to understand the concept of foreground and background. One eight year old did a castle in the background and cut out a large bird on a branch for the foreground. It was spectacular!

Who do you think this famous person is?

Drawing Father Christmas/Santa, Sculpting Father Christmas:

If you choose to make a **three dimensional** Father Christmas, you can use an apple for the head. Peel the apple and cut out the core. Stuff the core area with cotton. Carve eyes, nose and mouth into the apple. The areas you carve will look deeper as the apple dries. Dip the apple into lemon juice and cover it with salt. Put the apple in the oven at 100 degrees and then let it dry for a week. Wash, dry and shellac your apple. Add eyes, nose, beard, lips, etc. You now have the head of Father Christmas, **three-dimensional art.** Add a hat and collar and cotton for hair. Thomas Nast was the first artist to draw a picture of Santa Claus as we visualize him today. Go to this website to see an example. <http://en.wikipedia.org/wiki/Thomas_Nast>.kkkk

Use the diagram below when you do your picture of Father Christmas.

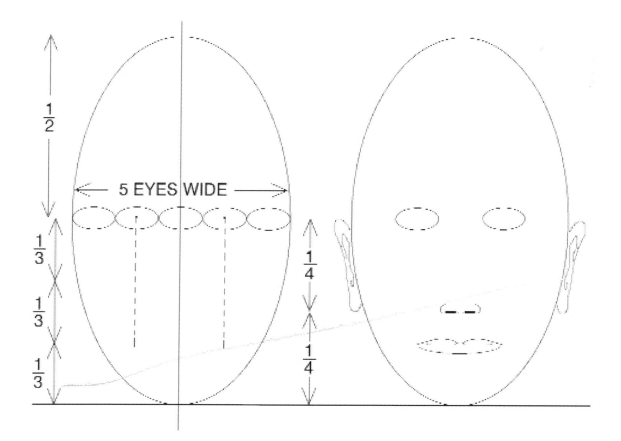

How do costume designers know how to dress people of different time periods? Before the development of the camera, artists pictured history. Benjamen West was appointed the historical artist to the court of King George. When you look at the details on the people's clothing above left, you can see a sword, a crown, shoes, different kinds of fabric, etc. The picture above left is from between 1861 and 1890. The original artwork was in color. The time period is from the 6th to the 10th century. Above right is a reproduction of a painting done by Rembrandt, a Baroque artist. Since this was in the 1700's, we can look at the clothing and get an idea of what well dressed men wore at the time. Choose a character from one of Tolkein's or C.S. Lewis's books and design clothing for them to wear.

The picture on the left has not been redrawn by modern artists. It was found in one of the earliest printed books, between 1475 and 1500. Pictures are found from *Aesop's Fables; Mandeville's Travels*, and the *Hortus Sanitatis*, a favorite book of medical instructions and natural history. Many were woodblock prints. We can realize what type of clothing was worn during this time period by looking at these pictures. The famous painting "Mona Lisa" lets us know what ladies of her time period dressed like.

Take a basic shape for a robe from the picture above and design a robe for a king or queen to wear who reigned in this ancient kingdom. Notice the dragons ond the robe above. Notice the use of patterns. An **arabesque** is a complex and elaborate design made of many lines. Do you see any of these designs above?

Props for Your Story

A story about an ancient land needs **props**. Musical instruments were primitive. Have students create simple instruments from strings and cardboard and rubber bands. Have students look up the word lyre. What instruments were mentioned in some of the Bible stories?

Pottery is important because ancient people needed ways to carry their food and drinks. A good project with students is to go to your local discount store and purchase terra cotta pottery in the garden center. Allow students to draw a design on a pot with lots of patterns similar to the one on the left. When finished, let them paint it with acrylic paint.

The picture below is a wood block print from the 1500's. Doing a print is easy if using a foam meat tray. Cut off the sides and use a pencil to indent a design in the tray. When you are finished, rub black paint over the tray. Print on paper until the right consistency is achieved and you have a print similar to the one below. You can use a variety of colors to color your print.

FOAM MEAT TRAY

CUT OFF THE SIDES OF THE TRAY

USE A BLUNT PENCIL TO INDENT THE FOAM

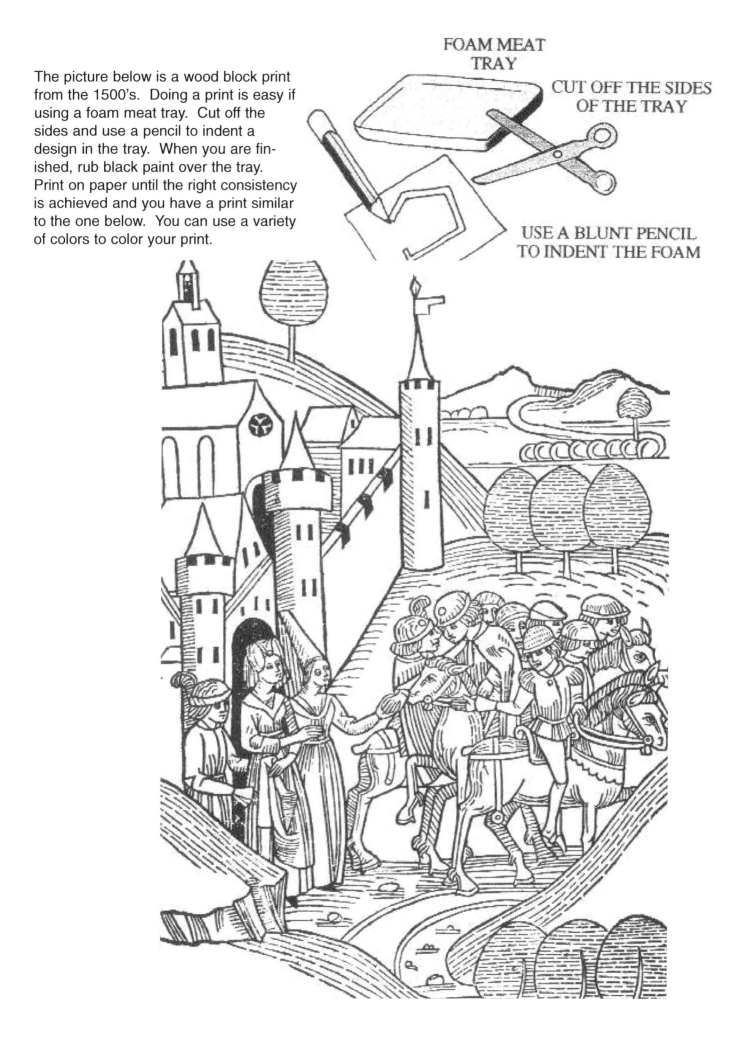

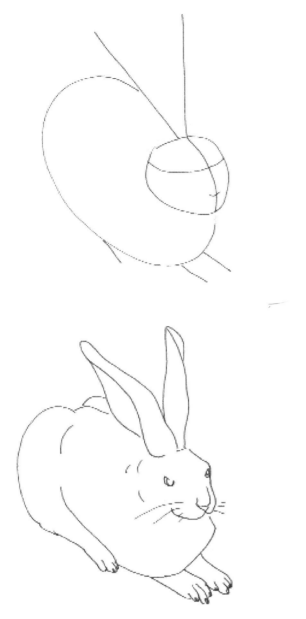

All the animals in Narnia and other fantasy stories were talking animals. In many other fantasy stories, the animals have human characteristics. How could you make this rabbit look like it could talk? What could you do to make it look more human? On the left is a very famous picture of a rabbit by Durer, an artist of the German Renaissance. Go to this website to see his most famous painting "Praying Hands."
<http://www.artchive.D/durer_praying_hands.jpg.htm>

Wildlife art is one of the most popular forms of art today. The beavers in Narnia all spoke English. It is said that Disney got his idea for Mickey Mouse while drawing at the zoo; and that Disney artists of today study real animals to make their creations. Making up cartoon art requires the use of **exaggeration** and **sterotyping**. Look up both of these words in the dictionary. Make a beaver for a comic strip. Decide what your beaver will be and then use sterotyping to dress him up.

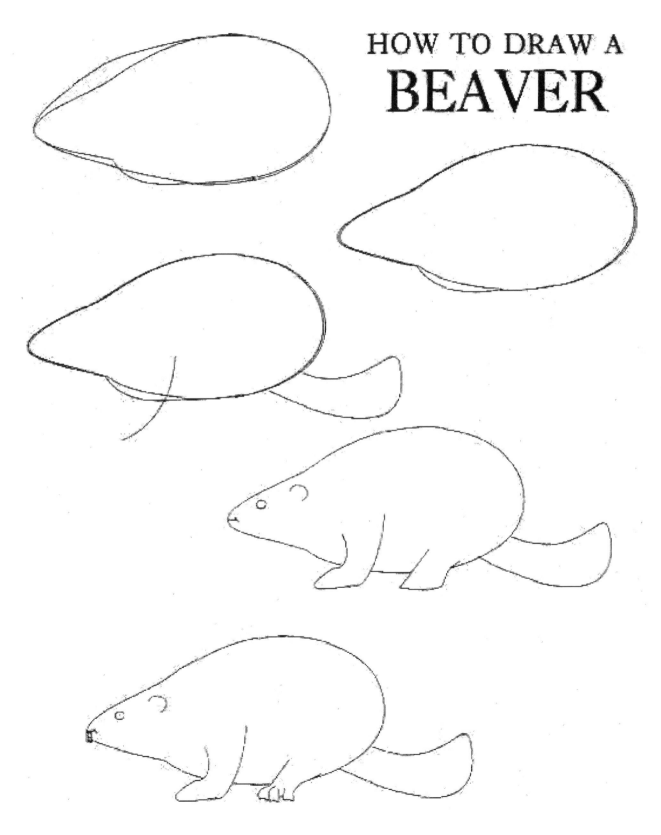

HOW TO DRAW A
BEAVER

Draw your beaver similar to the one in the space below. How can you make it look like it could speak in our language?

The name faun was made up because of part human and part animal characteristics. The character is part human and part goat. Make up a character that is part human and part beaver. Give your character a name and then draw something in his hands/paws that tells us something about him. Name your character.

Gargoyles

These grotesque creatures were supposed to frighten away the evil spirits. They remind me somewhat of the scarecrows of today. True **gargoyles** are water-spouts, taken from the French word "throat." They usually project from the gutter of the top of a building. They are seen in many of the older European cathedrals and other structures. Here are some examples.

Design your own gargoyle below around a mouth. Know that it will have water coming out of its mouth when it rains.

This "Green Man" appears on a cathedral in France called Cathedral of Saint-Etienne. Can you imagine having a figure like this as part of your roof? Make a figure out of leaves similar to the one above. Perhaps C.S. Lewis or other fantasy writers got some of their ideas about turning things into stones by looking at European cathedrals.

A **griffin** is a mythical creature with the body and head and of a lion and the head wings, and claws of an eagle. Practice drawing the lion body and then draw the head and wings of an eagle.

Narnia/Middle Earth Money

If you were assigned to make money for a mystical country, what animal would you put on the coins? Why?

CAPT. HERBECK
ENTERS THE LIONS DEN
AT EVERY PERFORMANCE
AT THE RISK OF HIS LIFE.
YOU WILL NEVER FORGET
THIS PERFORMANCE

In early American history, the circus was one of the most popular methods of entertainment. The lion act was always an important part of the entertainment. Look at the way these lions are positioned. Diagonal lines always show movement in art. You can draw these lions using basic circles lightly in pencil first. You can draw a picture of a lion jumping by using this lion as an example. Look at the shape of the body. See if you can see circles and ovals in the shape. Define your space using basic shapes and then use shading, shadow and texture to make the lion look like he is moving.

When you start drawing trees, you need to remeber that you start with a thick trunk and then make the branches thinner and thinner; there are all different kinds of the letter Y. When the season is winter, you don't need to add leaves. When you do your trees, be sure to put expressions on their faces. How could you make a tree look like a spy? Draw a tree on white paper then draw one at night on black paper as the example on the following page has been done.

The white is **postive space** and the black is **negative space.**

You can do straw painting on blue paper, it will look like the picture on the right. Use black tempera paint and blow it on the paper using a straw. Do not inhale. Let dry and put a bird on the tree.

Can you see the eyes and mouth on this tree? Does it look like it is spying on you? When you give something that is not human human characteristics, that is called **personification**. Look at the diagram on the right. Take a whole sheet of brown construction paper or a brown paper bag and cut a door out. Glue this on a large piece of white paper and let them draw the inside of a house in the tree. It is a home for a squirrel.

Draw a squirrel for the finished tree using the directions on the following page.

41

Squirrels in Narnia:

When drawing an animal, find a picture that you like. Block out your space with basic shapes. Modify the shapes and use shading, shadow and texture to finish the picture. Where is the light coming from in the following picture? Draw the leopard on the right using this technique. Leopards have appeared in many fantasy stories throughout history.

Finish the two leopard heads above.

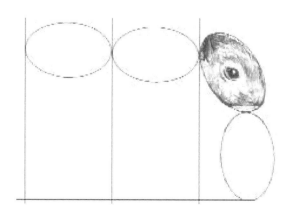

There have been many stories about hunting the milk white stag in literature. Can you see elements of feeling in the picture above? What is the **mood** of the picture?

Create a picture on black paper of feasting and joy in the forest of Narnia before the white witch. Remember the black is **negative space** and the white is **positive space.**

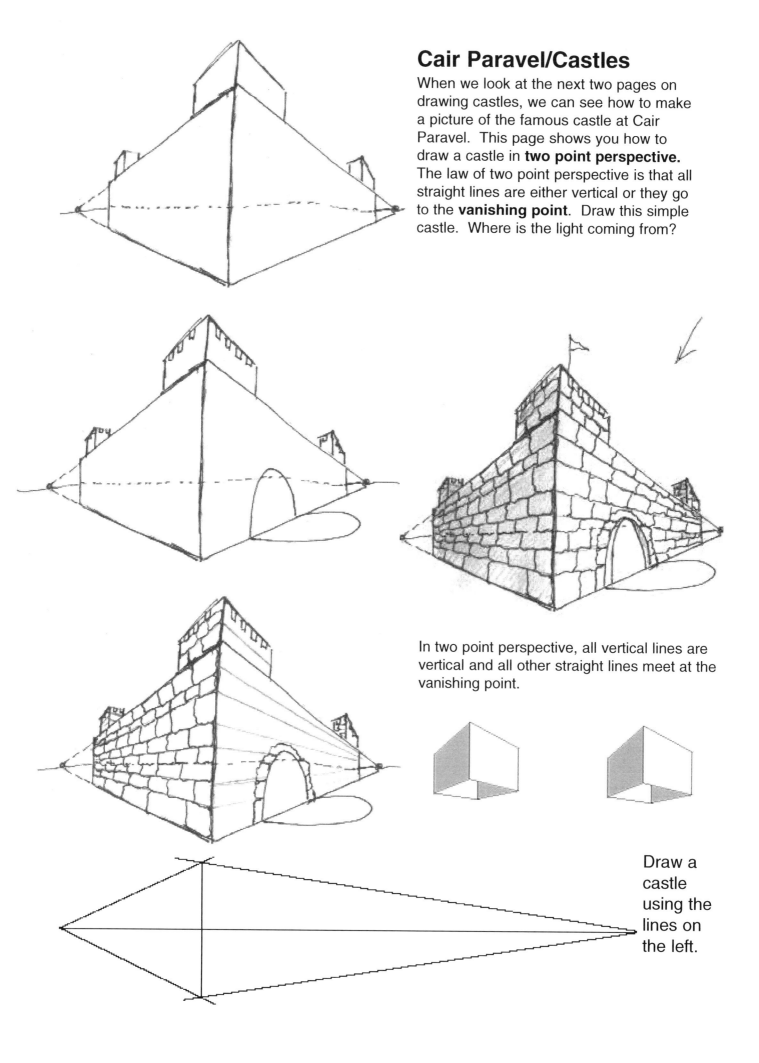

Cair Paravel/Castles

When we look at the next two pages on drawing castles, we can see how to make a picture of the famous castle at Cair Paravel. This page shows you how to draw a castle in **two point perspective.** The law of two point perspective is that all straight lines are either vertical or they go to the **vanishing point**. Draw this simple castle. Where is the light coming from?

In two point perspective, all vertical lines are vertical and all other straight lines meet at the vanishing point.

Draw a castle using the lines on the left.

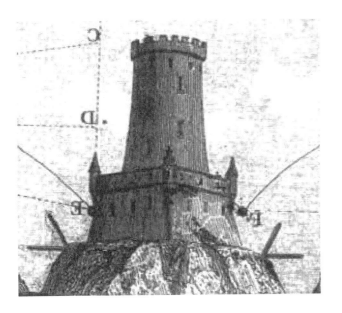

The picture on the left could be a good portion of the castle. Where is the light coming from in the picture? **Crenulations** are the top of the battlements. The notches were used for the archers when doing battle. It is an element of architecture.

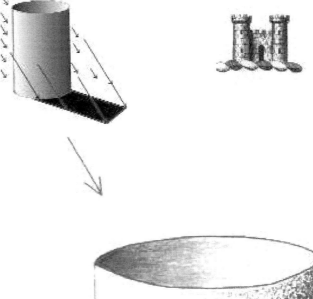

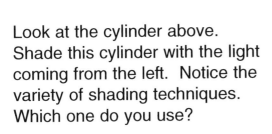

Look at the cylinder above. Shade this cylinder with the light coming from the left. Notice the variety of shading techniques. Which one do you use?

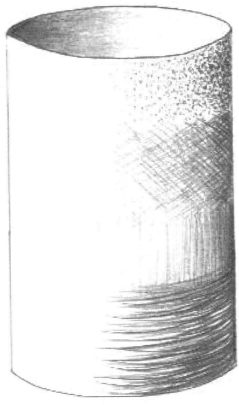

You can make a wonderful three dimensional castle out of sugar cubes. You can also make one out of coffee clay. See recipe on the following page.

Can you recognize where the light is coming from in the picture above? Can you tell where it is coming from in the castle below? Build a castle using Coffee Clay. It will be **three-dimensional art.** Draw the castle above using just shades of blue, black and white. Make it look like it is covered in ice and snow. This is a **monochromatic** color scheme. You can do the picture on blue paper. It will look cold and unappealing.

Coffee Clay
1 cup of flour (250 ml)
1/2 cup of salt (125 ml)
1 cup used coffee grinds (250 ml)
1/2 cup cold, left over coffee (125 ml)
Combine all these ingredients into a bowl
and stir until well blended.

Gather the mixture together with
your hand and knead on a floured
surface until our dough is very
smooth. Let air dry or bake at 175
for 30 minutes. Make into stone
shapes.

Birds can seem to give very powerful messages and to tell directions. I have heard several stories about after a death in the family God sent a bird to give comfort.

Drawing birds is very simple. You just use basic shapes and then detail. The birds on the upper left are field drawings by the famous bird artist David Plank. For little children, drawing birds on blue paper is a good way to get good results. Allow them to draw the birds and then use white tempera paint for the snow. They can use a Q-tip to get it to look like it is snowing!

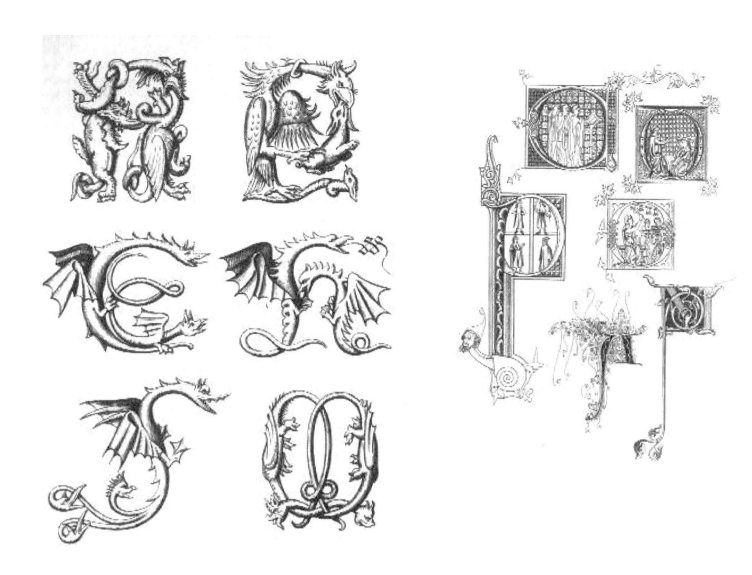

If you were writing a letter in Narnia or Middle Earth, what would the letters look like? The letters above are examples of ancient or medieval writing. Write the word ASLAN in Narnian dialect. Would your letters look like the ones above?

A **still life** is a grouping of inanimate objects. Bread throughout all of history has been a staple for modern and ancient peoples. Honey is another common food.

Nuts, grains, fruits, vegetables, etc are all things that are common. Design a table that might have been set in Narnia or Middle Earth. A **set designer** would do this when making a movie.

The next time you go to see a movie, notice the **props** that the actors use. These are designed by a **set designer**. Notice the credits that appear at the end of the movie.

Draw a box of Turkish Delights and a hot drink. At the right and bottom are candies that could be in the box. How can we show the true evil that is in the goodies? Look at the picture on the next page as an example. Did the artist make the cake look like it was not any good? Sometimes things that we eat look very good, but in fact are not good for us at all. If the Turkish Delights looked like the evil things they really were, and that they would lead Edward into terrible trouble, he would never have eaten them. Draw something that you think tastes good but is in reality very evil for you.

Foods that might have been eaten in ancient times are apples, berries, honey, breads, etc.

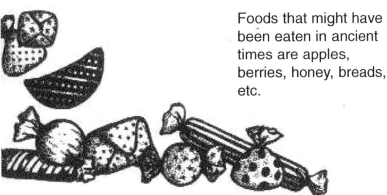

Do you think the artist made this piece of cake look like it would be good to eat? He might have made it very appealing but he did not. How could you make Turkish Delight look like the evil thing that it really was?

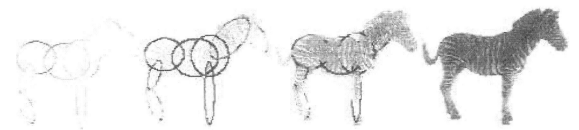

When you learn to draw animals that have fur, you need to learn how to do **implied texture**. Younger children can feel a piece of fake fur, or pet their cat or dog and get the concept of **texture**. But as children get older, they can create an implied texture with their pencil. These animals above not only have fur, but they have **patterns** or repeated designs on their fur. Create a picture frame like the one above using animals that have fur and also have patterns on their fur.

Showing Scale

In the dragon picture on the upper right, we can see the size of the dragon in relationship to the knight. The picture is done on black paper. Use light colors and make a knight and dragon on black paper. The black is **negative space** and the light is **positive space.** The picture above and on the left are examples of dragons where you can know their size by looking at the other object in the picture. This is called showing **scale** in a picture.

52

The dragon on my left is my favorite way to teach how to draw a dragon to young people. Of course, you need to add **shading, shadow and texture** to get it to look real. We can look at reptiles of today and get the idea of what the skin of a dragon/dinosaur might look like. We even have the komodo dragon of today to look at for ideas. For wee little ones draw the dino below in the water.

Have students show **implied texture** by putting the scales on the skin of the dragon.

Ancient Maps of Middle Earth/Narnia/Fantasy Places

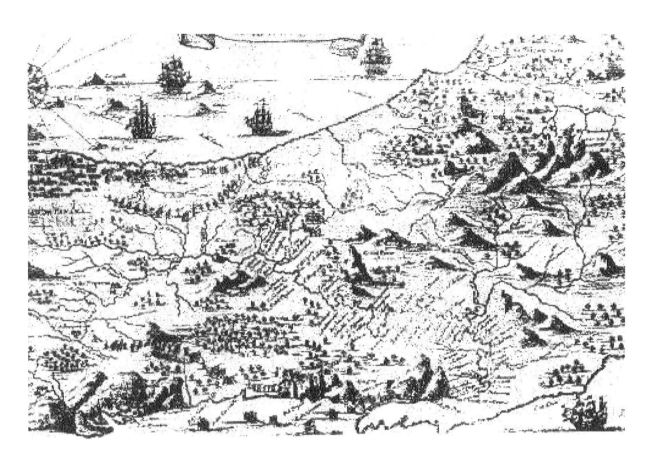

Cartography is the wonderful art of mapmaking. Making a map for an ancient country is quite a task. How can you get the map to look old? Will you make it out of papyrus or perhaps clay? Go to this website and see examples of maps of old <http://www.henry-davis.com/MAPS/Ancient%Web%20Pages/Ancient>.htm>. You can also do a search under "ancient maps" and find many websites with examples. Use your imagination and try to make the map look very old. Some suggestions are to soak paper in tea; use a brown paper bag and tear the edges. Soak it in soapsuds and microwave it. You can use a brown paper bag and wad it up and spend time making it look old by tearing the edges and crumpling it. See if you can make a map of Middle Earth and then Narnia and make them look very old. You can even put them in a frame and put it on the wall if you are pleased with it!!!

When you want to draw a unicorn, you start with the shape of a horse.

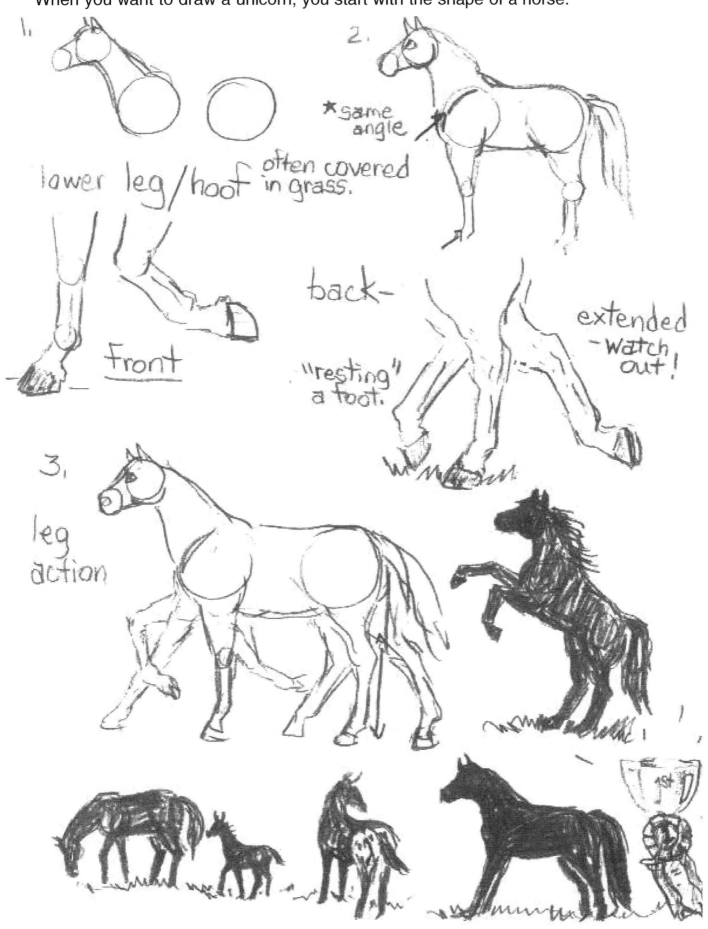

1.

★ same angle

lower leg/hoof often covered in grass.

2.

Front

back-

"resting" a foot.

extended -watch out!

3.

leg action

Set designers make sketches similar to the one on the left to get an idea of what an actor would wear. To make a unicorn, just add a horn to the center of the horse's head. Horses were dressed in battle arrray similar to the brave knights. Use your imagination and design a unicorn and dress him in battle armor.

Draw your unicorn in the space below.

Create a Kingdom

When you study about ancient kingdoms such as Greece and Egypt, do you get any ideas of what life might have been like there? An ancient kingdom named Narnia did actually exist in history.

A good creative idea is to create and name your own kingdom. This has been done many times. After Walt Disney created Mickey Mouse, he then created Disneyland. The wonderful character of Charlie Brown was created and all his friends were added. These characters taught us many valuable lessons of life.   Many people believe C. S. Lewis wanted to tell the story of Jesus and did it in a novel way. They believed he used the story *The Lion, the Witch and the Wardrobe* to do so.

Use your own creative powers and think of a message or story you want to tell. Create original characters and a kingdom (**setting**), in which they will live. Tell the story and then create ways to advertise it. This means you tell others and promote your story. You could put pictures of your characters on bags, on calendars and even turn the characters into dolls. You can invent a game all about your story. Be sure to copyright your ideas. Put a small "c" with a circle around it and a date somewhere in the picture.   Be sure to put your name or initials beside it.

These are horns that welcome you into this imaginary new kingdom!

MORE BOOKS FROM VISUAL MANNA

Art Through the Core series...
> Teaching American History Through Art
> Teaching Astronomy Through Art
> Teaching English Through Art
> Teaching History Through Art
> Teaching Literature Through Art
> Teaching Math Through Art
> Teaching Science Through Art
> Teaching Social Studies Through Art

Other Books...
> Art Adventures in Narnia
> Art Basics for Children
> Bible Arts & Crafts
> Christian Holiday Arts & Crafts
> Dragons, Dinosaurs, Castles and Knights
> Drawing, Painting and Sculpting Horses
> Expanding Your Horizons Through Words
> Indians In Art
> Master Drawing
> Preschool & Early Elementary Art Basics
> Preschool Bible Lessons
> Visual Manna 1: Complete Art Curriculum
> Visual Manna 2: Advanced Techniques

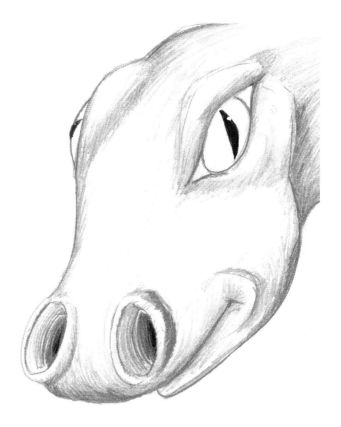

A Christian is one whose imagination should fly beyond the stars. Francis Schaeffer

Contact *visualmanna@gmail.com* if you are interested in our Intern program. Students learn how to teach art, do murals for ministry, prepare an excellent portfolio, and much more. Go to **visualmanna.com** for information.

Free art lessons are available at **OurHomeschoolForum.com** and books are available at Rainbow Resource Center (**www.rainbowresource.com**). Try all our "Art Through the Core" series and other books as well! Make learning fun for kids!!! Sharon Jeffus teaches Art Intensives in person for the Landry Academy at **landryacademy.com**.

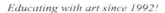

Educating with art since 1992!

Made in the USA
San Bernardino, CA
14 June 2016